Claude R. Buchanan

Queens Riddle

A Comedy in Four Acts

Claude R. Buchanan

Queens Riddle
A Comedy in Four Acts

ISBN/EAN: 9783337104054

Printed in Europe, USA, Canada, Australia, Japan

Cover: Foto ©Thomas Meinert / pixelio.de

More available books at **www.hansebooks.com**

QUEEN'S RIDDLE.

A COMEDY

IN
FOUR ACTS
BY

CLAUDE R. BUCHANAN.

Grand Rapids, Michigan.
Published by C. R. BUCHANAN.
——1896——

QUEEN'S RIDDLE.

SYNOPSIS OF SCENERY.

DRAMATIS PERSONÆ.

❧⟨❀⟩❧

King Arthur,..................Nicholas J. Hoey.

Sir Florent,.................William A. Andersch.

Sir Gregory,................Hugh B. Cavanaugh.

Teacup,...........................Paul P. Davis.

Old Man,.........................John J. Lane.

Jack...............................John J. Lane.

Guinevere,......................Nellie McKee.

Vivien,......................Louise La Valliere.

Julia,..........................Theresa Goebel.

First Witch,......................Paul P. Davis.

Second Witch, ...John J. Lane.

Catherina,...................Adeleine M. Mills.

Witches, wizards, pages, attendants, peasants, ladies
of the Court, devil.

❧⟨❀⟩❧

Produced at Power's Opera House, Grand Rapids,
Michigan, April 22nd, 1896.

QUEEN'S RIDDLE.

ACT I.

Gardens of King Arthur.

Vivien.

A short time ago I was an humble damsel of the lake. Quickly I jumped to gentlewoman, then easily became a lady of the Court, second alone to Guinevere, and now I see my way direct to the Queen's robes! I will be Arthur's queen. Teach me, O Merlin, to be wise and cunning! (writing) "My dear G."— "Pardon my failure"—" to meet you here yesterday." —"I shall not fail to meet you at three."—"F." Those are his f's. his ss, his r's and y's. Anyone will say it is the handwriting of Florent. This note will set the King on fire. if he find it. (Drops the note.) And find it he will, for he is coming directly this way. How many a king is but a paltry slave! And he is mine.

[Exit.]—L. 1 E.
[King enters.]—R. U. E.

King. I'd give the richer part of all my kingdom to know—(Kicks note.) What's this? (Picks it up.) Eh? What do I see? (Reads.) "My dear G"— That means Guinevere! "Pardon my failure to meet you yesterday ; I shall not fail to meet you at three."— "F." Florent's own handwriting. At three! It is already three!

[Vivien enters.]—L. 1 E.

Viv. My Lord!
King. (Puts note quickly aside.) Vivien! Where is the Queen?

Viv. We lately parted—there she is with Florent!
(Points R. 2 E.)

King. Ah, as I thought!
I hold him, Vivien, a rogue, a trickster,
A janus-faced, unchivalrous humbug!

Viv. Why, what now, my lord?

King. If the rogue lays not siege to Guinevere—

Viv. Can you think so, my lord?

King. Call me most stupid, blind, a visionnaire—
And belike she loves him.

Viv. Why think you so?

King. Her eyes are ever dancing jigs with his.
At balls, at feasts, they never fail to meet.
One night I heard her cry in her sleep, "Florent!"

Viv. Our dreams they say, most go by contraries.

King. To-day I saw upon the inside cover
Of one of her choice books, in her own hand,
Scribbled as if in thoughtlessness, the names
"Florent and Guinevere." Is't not suspicious?

Viv. I know not what to say.

King. She dropped her handkerchief at our last
tourney.
Florent's quick eye saw it and brought it her.
Their coquetry that day lasted an hour.
So, Vivien, I do mistrust them both.

Viv. I've seen nothing amiss. She means no
harm.
I think her firm in her fidelity.

King. I'll hazard the richest gem within my
kingdom
That she's enamored of this Knight Florent.

Viv. I'll stake my hand against your precious gem
That she is true, unalterably true.
The honored head that wears a nations cares
Deserves all love an earthly queen can·give.
He whose hard labors, far away, bring joy
For those at home, his sweetest hours lost,
Deserves his lady's love when he returns.

King. And he who tricks him of it deserves damnation.

Viv. My lord, if I were Queen and loved another
I'd call my love a tumor, cut it out,
And dedicate anew the poor remainder
To serve my lord anew with purer love.
I do not think your Queen could love another.

King. Fair Vivien were fit to be a Queen.

Viv. I—I a Queen! Ha, ha, ha! I a Queen! A
Queen?
No, no, my lord! If your good Queen prove false,
Forswear the sex, that is not what it seems.
I a Queen! Ha, ha, ha! Perchance a mate for you?
Ha, ha!
Come, Arthur, listen while I give advice!
I pray you be not jealous, good my lord,
Until you have the proof before your eyes!

King. See then the proof. (Shows the note.)
Here is a note, read it.

Viv. (Reads.) Ah, this is strange! "To G" and
signed by "F."
And yet these grounds are open to the public,
And there are many "G's" and many "F's."
This argues nothing.

King. (Pointing) Are they not together,
And at the hour of three, the hour appointed?

Viv. I'll not believe it till before my eyes
I see them making love with many sighs.
But see, my lord, the Queen and Knight are coming!

King. Let us step back and stay here unobserved.

Viv. I do not like eavesdropping, good my lord.

King. Come, come!

Viv. Well, for the love I bear you, I will stay.

[King and Vivien retire up L.]
[Enter Queen and Florent.]—R. 2 E

Guin. Why am I choleric to-day? Because my good
lord goes moping, moping about, hearing nothing,
saying nothing, greatly troubled of late about some
weighty matter which he says is not for my ears.
Now, am I Queen and worthy of such treatment?

Flo. Indeed not.

Guin. When I was married, I thought I married
    Arthur.
But he's wedded to his people and his Knights;
He has no wife. I am his housekeeper.
I lighten evening hours
When he may have a brief month's respite home;
I sometimes chase away his melancholy;
The silent King—I sometimes make him prattle;
Grave as he is, I sometimes make him sportive.
But, he's wedded to his people.
When he's at home his mind is far away.
Life is too short to live with a mute man.

Flo. Gently, Madame, rate not your lord too
harshly. The cares of state annoy him, incessant war
follows close at his heels, with the loss of some of his
best Knights, slain or imprisoned.

Guin. Methinks it is none of these things.—

Flo. Then, belike it is some perilous quest, some
new adventure, or some new plot 'gainst his throne,
that torments him.

Guin. He hath little fear of these things.

Flo. —or dread of witchcraft, fear of enchanted
robes or magic horns, that bring discord and destruc-
tion to his court.

Guin. None of these things. I think, disturb him.

Flo. Then, belike, hath Cupid smitten him sore
and stolen away his senses.

Guin. Arthur in love? (Laughs.) He cares not
a whit for the whole female sex, and has no time to
love.

Flo. No time to love! Who has no time to love
Is either knave or fool.
All of us live to love and be beloved.
Damsel, knight, yeoman, peasant, queen and king,
All have their time and place and circumstance.
Each in their way, they love and have their lovers.
While your lord sulks, and thus forgets himself
And you, I'll proffer to be your knight,
If you do will it.
For while I live, our matchless Guinevere
Shall not go unattended, unadmired.

Guin. Thanks for your gallantry and knightly
  courtesy.
You have a silvery tongue I love to hear.
Flo. If Arthur heard you speak those words, dear
  Queen,
He would pluck out my tongue within an hour.
Guin. Not while I live will he pluck out that
  tongue.
Farewell! I must return.
            [Queen exit.]—R. 2 E.
Flo. Adieu! (Kisses her hand.)
            [Enter Gregory.]—L. 2 E.
Greg. Ah, here you are,
A number of our friends are cracking bottles
Of choice old Saxon wine—yonder in the arbor.
Come, sip a glass or two!
Flo.   I'll join you.
I have something to tell you, Gregory.
            [Exeunt.]—L. 2 E.
            [King and Vivien come forward.]
King. By heaven, I've heard enough!
Viv. 'Tis all her fault. I'll hate her from this
  hour.—
I had not thought of it until this moment.
Here is a handkerchief the queen just loaned me.
My eyes were full of dust and mine was missing.
'Tis strange she should forget this tender token.
You see the "F."—Alas, I pity you!
King. (King examines and crumples it, then thrusts
  in pocket.)
Her guilt is now past question. I'll be revenged!
Viv. Say absolutely nothing yet, my lord.
Patiently watch your opportunity.
We'll soon contrive some plan—
King. I feel the qualms of hell!—
Viv. —to be revenged on him, and cast her off.
'Tis best, Arthur, that this be kept most secret.
No one should know it saving you and me,
Until the time. Then let the world know it.

King. I'll cast her off!—And be revenged on him!
[Leaves.]—R. U. E.

Viv. Now let it work.   At last I've roused the lion.
And heaven, kind heaven,
Smile upon Vivien and make me Queen.
I do not often pray, so heed my prayer.
Grant, oh kind heaven, to make me Arthur's Queen.
I hear the rabble's shouts mount to the sky,
"Long live Arthur and long live Vivien!"
He says he'll be revenged.   I'll help him to it.
His sweetest, swiftest vengeance sure must be
To cast her off, and then to marry me.
I will contrive to let the King see more,
And by this coquetry I will dethrone her!
[Exit.]—L.
[Enter King and Teacup.]—R. 2 E.

King. Teacup, in all my reign I have not had a
whole month's rest.   The cares of state are heavy;
and when at last I return home for a few weeks, like
Ulysses, I must stand aside and see some miscreant
make suit to my Penelope.

Teac. Is it possible?

King. I, too, am culpable, for Merlin warned me
not to marry her.

Teac. What, Guinevere?

King. He named another damsel, but I told him
my heart was set on Leodogrance fair daughter, that
I would have no other.

Teac. What did Merlin say?

King. He heaved a fearful sigh; said she was too
beautiful; would put me to great sorrow; and mumbled
something about Sir Launcelot.   I do retain your ser-
vices.   (Pays him.)

Teac. Retain me?

King. This insolent cur, Florent, must leave the
realm.   Yet I would not banish him on mere suspicion,
or do aught that is dishonorable; I only seek ample-
most proof, and then to do full justice; and that I shall
do, whatever be the cost.

Teac. Yes, my lord.

King. Sift the case to the uttermost and then report to me.

Teac. I will, my lord.

King. If the knight be culpable in this, he may be guilty of some other offence, and, if so, we might prefer some other charge, exile him, prevent a mighty scandal in the realm, and I could privately deal with Guinevere as might seem best.

Teac. I understand, my lord.

King. Now will I find whether this Queen and recreant Knight have sold themselves to Satan. I will not damn the Knight and Guinevere until I prove that they have damned themselves. Tho' it be hard, tho' I do think them guilty, I'll hold them guiltless both until I prove it. Look you, Teacup!

Teac. Ay, my lord!

King. What think you Teacup, is the Queen handsome?

Teac. She looks most beautiful to-day.

King. I thought so once, that she was angel-fair; and now, her perfect features I see no longer. I only behold a deceiving eye, a borrowed beauty, a studied grace. In everything I see an imperfection. I do despise, I hate, I loath her, Teacup, I loath her!

Teac. My lord, do not take this misfortune too seriously.

King. Too seriously?—A month ago was peace, to-day, damnation.

Teac. I think, my lord, your Knight is culpable, but not your worthy Queen.

King. Prove it, Teacup, prove it, and a thousand pounds are yours! And I will scourge myself and do great penance, and achieve some mighty quest to atone for my fierce jealousy. And now you know your business. Have all your wits. Farewell!

      [King exit.]—R. 2 E.
      [Enter Vivien.]—L. 1 E.

Viv. Teacup, a word.

Teac. Certainly, madame.

Viv. I do retain you. (Pays him.)

Teac. Retain me?

Viv. To watch the Queen. Let me know when she comes, when she goes, and particularly what she says to Florent!

Teac. I will, madame!

Viv. They are carrying on a brisk flirtation, but the Queen is more to blame.

Teac. Ay, madame.

Viv. The King is mightily wroth with the Knight, too, and will have him banished. Now, do not delay, nor search too long; you know what's wanted; so like a true lawyer, make your testimony fit your case; you do not need much law, only a little testimony, a few hirelings. Watch him closely, and you'll soon trip him and forever ingratiate yourself into the good will of Arthur.

Teac. I will, madame.

Viv. You could force a quarrel with him, cudgel him for any trifle, arrest him on the slightest pretext, have a few friends by, and Arthur will banish him from the Kingdom.

Teac. I will, madame.

Viv. Let me see, I forgot to pay you.

Teac. I believe so. (Vivien pays him again.)

Viv. Breach of the peace, assault and battery, embracery, any misdemeanor or felony you can stumble upon, get enough charges in the complaint to make it serious, do not leave out felonious assault, and I'll trust the King to banish him.

Teac. I will, madame.

Viv. Pay your witnesses in advance. Here, I had forgotten the witnesses. (Pays him.) You understand your business. Have all your wits—not too scrupulous, not too scrupulous!

[Teacup and Vivien exeunt.]—R. and L.
[Florent and Gregory enter.]—L. 2 E.

Flo. A glorious tongue-loosener is wine.
Do you feel it?—I drank a trifle too much.
I'll tell you something, Greg, but first I warn you
Do not repeat a word! I am in love!

(SONG.)

I fear not the shrill-voiced trumpet's alarms,
I fear not the clangor of mighty arms,
I fear not the feuter of any lance,
Alas, I'm unhorsed by a maiden's glance!
   I love her!

Alas, what is this pricking me sore,
This painful thumping at my door
By night, by day? It is my folly
That both in mirth and melancholy,
   I love her!

Alas, can it not be that I,
While searching every nook I fly,
Shall chance some day her to espy,
Shall dare to tell her eye to eye,
   I love her?

If we should chance to meet some day,
I shall not quake and run away!
I'll dress me to her on the spot,
Tell a plain story, sir, why not?
   I love her!

Three days ago I passed a girl on the street.
I'd give half that I own to know her name.
  Greg. I'll take you at your word, half of your goods.
if I but learn her name. Make haste, describe her!
You have not learned whether her voice be sweet, her
intellect bright, whether she hath that exquisite grace
and general perfection which distinguish the inane
visage of a doll from a real woman.
  And how's her tongue? Wait till she starts that
    going!
There's many a maid I could devoutly love
If I had never seen her mouth in motion.
  Flo. I have no fear. Her tongue will be perfection.
  Greg. How are her eyes?
  Flo. Fine, large, lusterful, denoting great intelli-
    gence.
  Greg. How is her gait, not this modern dip, I hope.
    (Imitates.)

Flo. Lord, no! Straight as an arrow!
But Gregory, her glance! Oh Ceres, Minerva, Venus!
Why, she will drive me mad! I cannot sleep!
I have set eyes on one I know to be
Fairer than Egypt's Queen or Leda's daughter!

Greg. Who is that yonder?

[Julia appears in background,]—R. U. E.

Flo. As I live, 'tis she!

Greg. Well, do not rush off to her, fool!

[Julia crosses stage in background. Exit.]
—L. U. E.

For heaven's sake man, let her alone!

Flo. Dear Greg, let go! Excuse me for today.
I'll find out who she is without delay. [Exit]—L. U. E.

Greg. Venus is the breeder of more lunatics than
all the other gods combined!

(Laughs.) Assuredly, I was a fool to give Florent
the wine!—
A fool in love will hit reproof in the eye,
Tweak judgment by the ears, scorn doubt, and dash
His brains against impossibility!
But love and wine combined make him stark mad.
He'll go to jail without me! [Exit.]—R. 2 E.

[Re-enter Julia, followed by Florent.]—
L. U. E.

[Teacup and others appear at sides with
sticks.]

Flo. Pardon me, girl.

Jul. Certainly. What was it, sir?

Flo. You know me, Sir Florent?

Jul. Ay, sir, I know of you as being a right valiant
Knight.

Flo. I have a word to say, but know not how to
say it.

Jul. If you will give me your thought, I think I
have a ready tongue that will express it.

Flo. Well then, in brief, if you were in love with a
Sir Knight, how would you have him woo you?

Jul. (Laughs.) Knowing you, sir, to be a valiant
Knight, and true and honorable, I will tell you truly.
For I see, sir, you are sorely in love with some fair girl.

Well, sir, I would have him take me by the hand,
thus, and whisper in my ear, "I love you." Then,
sir, would I have him kiss me! (Laughs and starts to
leave.)

Flo. Wait! Methinks you are a girl of no little
wit. What is your name?

Jul. My name. sir, is Julia.

Flo. Now, Julia, is that all you would have the
Knight do?

Jul. Nay, after that let him say whatever love
would prompt him to say.   (Starts to leave.)

Flo. Wait! I beg you teach me further. Now,
first I take your hand, then whisper in your ear, "I love
you," then—(Kisses her.)

Jul. Oh. sir—

Flo. I'm practising, and must not omit one single
detail.

Jul. You are a very apt pupil, sir, for an amateur.

Flo. If I act well, then I pray you teach me further.

Jul. I fear I cannot. Your gestures, carriage, and
voice are excellent.

Flo. Then I may hope to win my lady. Now tell
me what to say to her.

Jul. Always speak as the heart may dictate, and
you will win your way straight to her heart.

Flo. Then that part I can perform without a
prompter. Julia, I cannot leave until I say I've never
met a maid of half your worth.

Jul. (Laughs) You are no amateur, sir, you are
an old actor, and I fear you're somewhat given to
flattery.

Flo. Nay, not a bit. I speak the very truth. And
now. by knightly honor, I make oath, you are the very
first that I have loved!

Jul. Oh, what a fib!

Flo. 'Tis true!

Jul. You are merry to-day, sir.

Flo. I am most serious.

Jul. I fear you came to mock me.

Flo. No, no! Believe me when I say, I think
You're proof that heaven still visits earth,
That gods in happy seasons mingle here.

Jul. Am I a goddess then? (Laughs.)

Flo. Yes, you are a goddess.
Never has the queen of love in heaven or earth
Watched the soft slumbers of a fairer brow.

Jul. (Draws away.) You would not marry such
    as me. Sir Knight,
And would you trifle with an humble girl?
They say that noble knaves ascend to gods,
But what's more pitiable than a woman wronged?
Go, find some lady of the court, Sir Knight.
You are courtier, sir, a Knight, a warrior,
You're known and honored all the country over.
How can you marry me, a peasant girl,
Undowered, humble, fatherless and poor?

Flo. I'll make you lady, or renounce my office.
I'll be your father and your husband too.
My dearest girl, I love you from my heart.
                        (He embraces her.)
            [Teacup, Punch and Jack come forward. |

Teac. (Strikes him on left shoulder.) What is the
    trouble, sir?

Flo. Trouble?

Jack. (Strikes him on right shoulder.) Yes, what
    difficulty?

Flo. Difficulty?

Teac. We regret this affair, sir.

Flo. Regret what?

Jack. Yes, we are sorry.

Flo. Sorry for what?

Teac. This trouble. (Beat him.)

Flo. Away!—Know you not me, I am Sir Knight
Florent? What mean you, churls, by this insolence?
I'll treat you all as worthless, drunken brawlers. Come
on. I give you leave to strike. (Advances. They
scatter.) Come, rogues, off with you. You've carried
this practical joke far enough. Come, be off.
(Advances. They scatter.)

Teac. Help ho! Hello! Help ho! Murder!

Jack. Help ho, Murder!

[Ragamuffin crowd enter.]
[All three advance boldly. Teacup strikes
him on shoulder.]

Teac. We arrest you, sir, in the name of the King!

Flo. Me? Florent? This is some great blunder,
sir, and it is a rank disgrace to be dragged before the
King.

Teac. Sir, you must balance this account with the
King.

Flo. Produce your warrant.

Teac. (Three confer together.) No warrant is
necessary. You have committed a breach of the peace
in the presence of the officer.

Flo. What breach?

Teac. I will not argue it, sir. Also assault and
battery, sir.

Flo. Assault on whom?

Teac. On the girl, of course. Also, embracery, sir.

Flo. Embracery? Have I been attempting to
corrupt judge or jury?

Teac. Who said anything about judge or jury, sir?
You have been clasping a girl in your arms, laying on
your hands in a circum-stantial manner, which is a gross
misdemeanor. a felony. So is resisting an officer. and
all other acts against the peace of the King and the
laws of the realm. But we are not trying you, sir, we
are arresting you.

Flo. Rogues, I'll be revenged.

Teac. How?

Flo. By catching and cudgelling each one of you
within an inch of your lives.

Teac. Are you an artistic cudgeller?

Flo. Watch! For as sure as to-morrow's sun rises,
I will some day catch you and give you such a trounc-
ing as—

Teac. You catch and cudgel me? You? Me?
Ha, ha!

Flo. Would you prefer hanging?

Teac. I saw him lately hanging by the neck, and I call him a poor hangman.

Flo. Come, let us be serious. You talk of breaches, assaults, misdemeanors and felonies, that I have wronged the girl. The girl acquits me of the charge, do you not?

Jul. Certainly, I do acquit him.

Flo. You know my lineage. You know I fought with Arthur against the Gauls and Romans. Think you today I've suddenly turned knave, that you today should disgrace me before the King? When I was page, my mother taught me courtesy, modesty, obedience, respect, love and reverence for womankind, and think you I would insult a woman? And, when at twenty-one, my sword was blessed and hung about my neck, and I was given spear, helmet, shield and spurs, and Sir Launcelot du Lake, that flower of all knighthood smote me on the neck and dubbed me a Sir Knight, I swore by St. Michael and St. George forever to be a protector of womanhood, especially the widow and the orphan, and think you I would insult an orphan maid? Come, let us part friends, and call this day's circumstance a capital joke.

(Extends his hand to Teacup.)

Teac. 'Twill be a most serious joke, for you must appear before the King.

Flo. The direst disgrace that can befall a knight is a notorious arrest and an arraignment at the King's palace. You smirch my honest name, tarnish my Knighthood, bandy my name about the realm as a common brawler arrested by a common petty constable and his parasites: disbar me from the court; disfranchise me from the fellowship of the Knights of the Round Table. Come, are you men or are you hirelings?

Teac. You must settle this, sir, with the King.

Flo. Very well. Fall into line! I will lead the van. Let the ragamuffins and scullions come next; then the rogues and hirelings; then the imbeciles and poltroons. Let the buffoons and idiots come last. I will abide the law, and one and all, I defy you. I'll trust my case to Arthur.

Curtain.

ACT II.

Audience room of King. Throne. King seated. Pages on either side of King. Teacup, Punch, Jack, Florent and Julia discovered.

Teac. Hear ye, the Court of Arthur, King of Britain, subduer of Saxons and Germans. conqueror of Ireland, Iceland, Norway and Gaul, is now in session.

King. What is the complaint?

Teac. (With paper.) Charge one: A disturber of the public peace. in a public quarrel with a peasant girl, one Julia, in the public gardens of your honor. Second charge: Embracery. or the act of putting ones arms around a person of the opposite sex. 'Tis certainly a grievous and heinous offense to put ones arms about a girl. but. strange to say, I find no statute against this kind of embracery, doubtless because the thing is so rare; possibly because such a thing never occurred before. But embracery is a gross misdemeanor, is it not, your honor?

King. You confound embracery and embracement.

Teac. Is there any difference?

King. Embracery is an attempt to influence a jury, court, etc.. corruptly, by promises, persuasions, entreaties, money, entertainments or the like. What you mean is embracement, which is a clasp in the arms, a hug, an embrace. and is one of the rankest offenses known to the common law, subjecting the offender to heavy fine. imprisonment, and even expatriation. Proceed with the complaint.

Teac. Third charge: Osculation, or the act of kissing a person without special request. The reported cases are very rare. sire, but this offense is prohibited in any form, there being three forms: involuntary osculation, osculatory insinuation and osculatory enforcement. Involuntary osculation, as where a lady throws a kiss to a Sir Knight without his consent, or a Sir Knight to a lady without her consent; fine, five to ten pounds, according to the vexation. Osculatory insinuation, as where a lady steals a kiss from a Sir Knight, or a Sir Knight steals one from a lady partly without consent, and wholly without invitation; fine, ten to fifty pounds, according to the aggravation. In Gareth v. Elaine, et al., the 5th of Arthur, page 42, three ladies had the audacity to approach the Knight on the street and kiss him before he could run away, and thereupon, the Knight, very much abashed, and blushing deeply, made complaint to your honor, swore out a warrant, had them arrested, and notwithstanding their protests and entreaties, your honor fined them each fifty pounds and costs. Lastly, osculatory enforcement, as where a Sir Knight kisses a lady violently and against her will, which is the case at bar, is punishable by a fine of one hundred to five hundred pounds, according to the provocation. In the 6th of Arthur, page 62, a Knight was fined two hundred pounds for kissing a girl. The fourth charge is assault and battery. The fifth, felonious assault. Sixth, grievous and aggravated blasphemy. Seventh, resisting an officer. Eighth, a civil action will lie against the Knight for heavy punitive or exemplary damages for the injured feelings of the girl, the wounded pride, indignity, insult, mortification and humiliation.

King. What say you, Florent?

Flo. If the court please, not guilty. Some enemy of mine has trumped up these false charges.

King. Who are the complainant's witnesses?

Teac. We six.

King. Proceed with your testimony.

Teac. We caught the Knight in the act of assaulting the girl in the public gardens.

Flo. The rascal lies.

King. How is it, men?

Crowd. True, your honor.

Teac. They exchanged blows; was it not so?

Crowd. True, true.

Teac. She was trying to bite him in the face, and he was choking her as we rushed in.

King. How is it, men?

Crowd. True, your honor.

Teac. He also swore most foully, attempted to bribe us, and after we had arrested him in your Majesty's name, assaulted us, producing wounds about our heads and bodies as your honor sees.

Flo. My lord, I think some devil has suborned these fellows to traduce me. I used no blasphemy, made not the slightest suggestion of a bribe, never struck them a blow, nor did I wrong the girl in word or deed.

King. What say you, Julia?

Jul. What the Sir Knight has said is true.

King. Men, does the girl speak true or false?

Crowd. False, false!

King. Can you vouch for her veracity? Have you known her long?

Flo. Not long.

King. How long have you been acquainted?

Flo. Only to-day. (Crowd jeers.)

King. What business had you with her, sir?

Flo. None, your honor, except—I was much taken with the girl. (Crowd laugh and jeer.)

Teac. Your honor, he laid hold of the girl, and said some vile thing, did he not?

Crowd. He did, your honor.

Flo. My lord, is this a trial, and must I stand abashed and silent before this crowd of parasites, hirelings and perjurers, whom some enemy of mine has hired to appear here and ruin me? Is not my word and that of the girl, good against this motley crowd?

King. You plead the general issue. Have you any special plea?

Flo. I plead fraud, conspiracy, subornation in the procurement of these charges. I further state, that being much taken with the girl, I asked her for her hand. I love the maiden. (Loud laughter and jeers from crowd.)

King. Your plea is put forth gingerly, I must say. Have you any other witnesses?

Flo. None, your honor.

King. Are all the eye witnesses of this affair here?

Teac. Yes, your honor.

King. Does the complainant rest?

Teac. We rest.

King. Does the defendant rest?

Flo. I rest trusting that your Honor will regard the word of a Knight and of an honest maid more highly than that of a hundred rogues.

King. The testimony stands six to two. You, Florent, and the girl are interested parties, and I must hold your testimony lightly. Here, I find six disinterested men, eye witnesses of the affair, and I must give their testimony great weight. True, you say they are hirelings, but until you prove them such, I must regard them as honest men. Florent, I needs must find you guilty of base conduct, an attack on the girl, the penalty of which cannot fall short of banishment from the realm.

> [R. 2 E.—Enter Queen who sits by side of King, and Vivien who sits at her feet.]

Flo. My lord, you cannot mean this!

King. The burden of proof rests heavily upon your shoulders. Florent, your guilt seems clear beyond exception, clear.

Jul. I pray you, let not your judgment on my account be so rigorous that the Knight must be banished. If you deem him guilty of any offense, I freely forgive and acquit him.

King. I judge him worthy of banishment, girl.

Jul. I pray you be lenient with him. No noble soul would censure you for sparing the Knight this disgrace.

Flo. Girl, for that kind word, a thousand thanks.

King. He is plainly worthy of banishment.

Jul. My gracious lord, to clothe thyself in the habiliments of pity, to spare the Knight this ignominy were an act worthy of a gracious sovereign.

Flo. Girl, I can never pay you what I owe.

King. I see you love this Knight.

Jul. I fear you love him not. But if you force me to it, some day I may put in a plea of guilty to that charge, and learn to love this Knight. But, your honor, I have heard that once in each year, all the Knights of the Round Table are solemnly sworn to show mercy to those who ask for mercy, and now we ask for mercy for this Knight.

King. What would you do if you were King, and deemed this Knight guilty of this offense?

Jul. Your honor, having discovered that this is a woman's case, I would transfer the matter to your most worthy Queen and to the female senate, and let the Council of the Queen decide it. (All laugh.)
[King, Queen, Vivien rise and move from their seats.]

Guin. What is the crime which calls for banishment?

King. He assaulted a maid and has disgraced his name,
Bringing reproach on me and on our court.
I swear I'll free our land from all such rogues.
No maid shall be insulted unavenged.

Viv. Is not a brief imprisonment enough?

King. Too light.

Guin. I doubt if he be guilty of aught else save indiscretion.

Viv. I, too, my lord. I beg you promise that this Knight shall stay.

Guin. Husband, you must.
I do implore, if still I have some share
Of that great love with which you wooed me once,
Spare us this Knight.

King. Why, Guinevere, I hear he has made suit
To one of the fair ladies of your court.
I hear his strong affection is returned,
But this same lady has a worthy spouse,
And would you have your court so scandalized?
Guin. Who, who is she?
King. I shall not give her name.
Viv. Believe no idle rumors, good my lord,
I do not think the Knight would stoop so low.
I hold your Knight Florent, one of the best
Who loves his lord, to serve him unto death.
Now, Arthur, hear our prayer we both implore,
Let him remain.   (Kneel.)
Guin. My gracious lord, since you have seen this is
A woman's cause,   (Kneel)
Therefore, I pray you, let our sex decide.
Let this case be transferred to the female senate.
Viv. Yes, let the Council of the Queen decide.
Guin. We'll sift the matter. We'll satisfy your
    lordship.
King. I leave this case with you on this condition,
That you and all the female court agree. (They rise.)
Not one dissenting vote. Your verdict must be
    unanimous.
I leave the case also on this condition,
That he shall roundly smart for this offense.
(Aside.)   These female juries always disagree.
        [Exeunt King and crowd.]—L. 2 E.
Guin. Vivien, go call the female court.
        [Exit Vivien.]—L. 2 E.
Flo. Here, madam, is the maiden.
Guin. Knight Florent, I hear, partook too freely of
wine, and as a merry prank made love to you.
Jul. He seemed most sober.
Flo. (Aside to Julia.) I was.
Guin. It was all a joke!
Jul. He seemed most earnest.
Flo. (Aside to Julia.) I was.
Guin. He loves another.

Jul. He spoke as if he loved me alone.

Flo. (Aside to Julia.) I do.

Guin. He would not marry one of your station.

Jul. He made me think he would.

Flo. (Aside to Julia.) I will.

[Slips hand behind her. Florent kisses it repeatedly.]

Jul. (Aside to Florent.) If you love me, why, say so to the Queen.

Guin. What is that?

Flo. (Aside.) Oh, what will come of this! (Steps between them.) Pardon me. I—I— (Aside to Julia.) The Queen thinks I am in love with her. (Julia and Florent laugh.) (Aside to Queen.) She still thinks I am in love with her, and perhaps I am. (Florent and Queen laugh.)

Guin. Oh—

Jul. Oh—

Flo. Oh— (All laugh together.)

[Enter Ladies of Court, with Vivien.]— R. 2 E.

Guin. Florentius's case, or rather persecution, has come to issue before my lord: a crowd of hirelings bore false witness, and the King summarily convicting him, has adjudged him worthy of banishment.

1st Lady. Is't possible?

2nd Lady. 'Tis cruel!

3rd Lady. 'Tis terrible!

Guin. I cannot understand the humor of my lord in this affair.

1st Lady. 'Twas too precipitate.

2nd Lady. He gave the Knight no time for his defense.

3rd Lady. Some jealous enemy seeks spiteful revenge.

Guin. But I have not delivered the news.

Ladies. News?

Guin. The case, by the clemency of my good lord, Has been transferred to the female court.

All. To us? (Laugh.)

Ladies. How did it come about? How did it happen?

Guin. This girl suggested it. (Laugh.)

2nd Lady. Methinks she is a girl of no little wit.

Guin. I esteem her highly. As for the Knight, I'll vouch for his veracity and innocence. The girl acquits him, do you not?

Jul. Most assuredly I do acquit him.

Guin. Now let us do full justice to the cause,
And win fair name and fame with all mankind.
All Britain will be waiting to learn our verdict.

1st Lady. The King has paid a great compliment to the Female Court.

Guin. Well, let us summon all our wit, wisdom and cunning, for we must outwit the King. I'll present this ring to the lady who can best tell us how we can save this Knight from banishment, for my lord says Florent must suffer for the offense, or leave the realm.

Flo. Tho' innocent, madame, I am willing to suffer any trial of Knightly skill, labor or hardship, that your fraternity may elect. So do what to your Female Court seems best. I will most cheerfully submit to your decision.

[Exit.]—R. 2 E.

1st Lady. This Knight, madame, is no culprit.

2nd Lady. Let him achieve the quest of the Holy Grail.

Guin. He would return like many other Knights, disgraced. If Launcelot has failed, can he accomplish it?

Lady. Let him slay the giant on St. Mighel's mount.

Guin. What, that monster that feeds on human babes; that wears the beards of fifteen vanquished Kings embroidered on his coat; that monster, that devil in human form. It were sure death.

Lady. No feat of arms will do.

Jul. I have heard, madame, that every Knight from Britain to Palestine regards trial by combat the highest tribunal for the settlement of guilt or innocence, of right or wrong. Am I correct?

Guin. Most certainly you are.

Jul. I have also heard that your code of female chivalry prizes a ready tongue and quick wit. Am I correct?

Guin. Indeed you are.

Jul. Then this occasion affords great opportunity to put your code of female chivlary to test. Instead of trial by combat, let the Knight have a trial of intellect.

All. Excellent! Excellent!

Guin. What trial shall he make?

Jul. Give him a riddle. (All laugh.)

Ladies. A riddle! A riddle!

Guin. What riddle shall we give him?

Jul. Ask him, "What do the women love the best?"

Guin. Yes, what do the women love the best, who knows?

Jul. You can make show of anger and severity,
And with dissembled hate you can declare
He shall be exiled if he fail to answer.
But the Female Court being his gentle judges
You can shout "Amen" to anything he says. (All laugh.)

1st Lady. Excellent.

2nd Lady. We have hit it.

3rd Lady. She is unsurpassed.

Guin. What if he hesitate?

Jul. Give him a year in which to solve the riddle.

Guin. One of you summon Florent. (Exit lady,) —R. 2 E. Another the King. (Lady leaves.)—L. 2 E. Here, Julia, take the ring. You have well earned it.

        [Enter Florent—R. 2, King—L. 2 E.]

King. Well, Guinevere, will you pass on the case?

Guin. (Mounting the throne.) Yes, my lord, I
    will.
Sir Knight Florent, though you deserve exile,
We'll spare you from that foredecreed disgrace.
Your home you now may ransom at a cost.

Flo. What is the cost, most worthy Queen?

        (Reaches for his money.)

Guin. We have a task for you to perform to gain your freedom.

Flo. I will gladly and quickly perform it, letting nothing stand 'twixt me and liberty and full acquittal. What is the task?

Guin. The task we give you is to solve an ancient riddle.

Flo. A riddle? I am not versed in riddles. Come, let me joust with the Knights of Arthur's Table Round, despatch me to some distant shore to rescue some fair maid from imprisonment, or let me avenge the death of some of our lost Knights. But do not shame me with some simple riddle, and make me the laughing stock of all mankind.

Guin. The Female Court have just decided that you must solve a riddle to gain your freedom.

Flo. What, then, is the riddle?

Guin. What is it, sir, that women love the best?

Flo. What does a woman love the best?

Guin. Ay, sir, what does a woman wish for most?

Flo. 'Tis love, I think, that women most desire.

King. Your reason, sir?

Flo. My reason is, life without love is naught.

Guin. Well said, Florent. My lord, a noble answer.

King. A noble answer? It's preposterous.
Why, love's a common marketable product.
'Tis daily bought and daily sold for a song.
An ounce of gold outweighs a ton of love;
And wealth, position, rank, how few have them;
The labor of a lifetime scarcely wins them.
Then, 'tis only now and then along the ages
That one is blessed with the wondrous gift of fame.
Thus fame, 'tis sure, outranks all other gifts.

Guin. My lord, you err in speaking for yourself.
Men may desire fame above all things,
But women all prefer a steadfast lover.
Fame, rank, position, wealth, may charm the men;
'Tis love that reigns supreme o'er female hearts.

King. What woman would not sell out at her price?

Guin. Shame, shame, my lord; you talk outrage-
ously.

King. What woman would refuse to mate a King?

Guin. There's many a one would scorn to marry
you.

Flo. Have you forgotten, King, a father's love?
Have you forgotten, too, a mother's love?
And know you not what filial love is, King?
And love of friend for friend, call that to mind.
And love of man for maid, know you not that?
As all our race hates death, so at the altar
Of life ascends one constant smoke of incense
In prayer to him who giveth us all life,
That we may live to love and be beloved.

Guin. The Knight is right,—what can you say to
that?

King. All trumpery,all hocus-pocus, Queen! Where
did you gather all this nonsense, sir?

Guin. No matter, Arthur, 'tis immaterial. We'll
settle this dispute without your help.

King. Well, ladies, let us hear. Is the Knight
right? Come, Clara, what think you?

Clara. I pray excuse.

King. Not so, out with it!

Clara. If I spoke for myself, I'd let love go and
take position and rank.

King. What say you, Kate?

Kate. I humbly do confess, I'd prefer wealth.

King. What say you, Vivien?

Viv. I'd much prefer honor and fame for mine.

Guin. Go, Knight, and search for a better answer.

Flo. Alas! I am no riddle solver, nor versed in
gypsies' art and magic.

Guin. Well, then you have a year to solve the riddle.
We give you leave to question all mankind.
If one year hence your answer be not given,
You shall depart, and all your goods be forfeit.

Flo. What one thing is it that women love the best?
Now have I struck a knot that is the toughest
That ever yet was tied.

What fool would ever think to ask a woman
What it would be that she would like the best?
Madame, the female heart I do not know.
    Guin. Then go and get acquainted with it, sir.
I pray you, sound it well. You will learn much.
    Flo. I fear, madame, my fate is foreordained;
That never again shall I see Camelot,
And never again behold the old familiar
Faces of this court. I am an outcast!
I'm in disgrace and shame and ignominy.
Come, let me joust with Arthur's valiant Knights
Until I reach my end and die a Knight.
    Guin. There's something greater than to die a
      Knight,
And that's to die a man.
Your first and highest duty is to be
Both to yourself and all mankind, a man.
I know you are a Knight, and valiant, too.
I know, sir, too, you are a gentleman;
But whether you be a man, ay, that's the question.
He who defies calamity and fate,
And with an arm of steel and heart of gold
Rises superior to fickle fortune.
Listens to conscience, intellect and God,
Him, him I would rejoice to dub a man.
Bestir thyself! Be a man and solve this riddle!
Curse not thy fate! Take courage, Knight Florent.
Thy fate is in thy hands, so fare thee well.
        [Queen and ladies exeunt.]—R. 2 E.
        [Florent sinks on seat.]—L. C.
           Curtain.

ACT III.

A wood. Dusk.

L. I. E.—[Enter Julia clad as a boy. An old man.]

Jul. Come, let us halt and rest an hour here.
(Sitting.)
I think they err. I fear that he has left.

O. M. Julia, come here. Look yonder. Who is
that?

Jul. Only another stranger. Note his cloak.
(Returns and reclines.)

O. M. This is the third time I have been deceived.
(Near her.) Poor girl, asleep! Poor rash and loving
thing!
I once could ford the loudest roaring stream,
And merrily mount up beyond the clouds.
I once could bear heat, cold, fatigue and hunger,
Hungrier thirst I could endure with joy
To reach that heaven built on woman's love.
As heaven dies with woman, mine is gone;
Soon I shall meet her in that far-off land.
At best, our heaven hangs on slender threads.—
How I have groaned, aching in every limb,
(Song, "What can an old man do but die?" Tom Hood.)
And yet this foolish girl makes no complaint.
The soul of woman in a frame of man
Had thrice two thousand years ago completed
The cycle of man's possibilities,
And would have turned to gods; as true they are.
This girl's attachment is most wonderful. (Goes to a
distance, reclines, and is soon asleep.)

[Florent clad as a monk and Gregory
enter.]—R- I. E.

Flo.   I know no human wit can solve the riddle.
I've traveled this broad land from coast to coast,
I've questioned all I've met. knocked at all doors.
I've asked the men, but chiefly I have questioned
Each woman, asking what she loved the best.
One said she loved great riches above all;
Another said position lofty; another power;
Another preferred honor; another chose merriment;
One widow pluckily said that she but hoped
To bury a dozen husbands 'fore she died.
Another prayed to be held chaste and wise.
One said 'twas her ambition to be praised
For her stability and secrecy.
One vowed she cared for nothing half so much
As to be fair and richly clad;
Another said that she were well contented
Could she be deemed of all among her sex
Perfection of a faithful, trusty housewife;
Another said, "Give me a right smart man.
I've hunted now some years to find a husband."
One said, "Oh, would that I were once more free
From the loathed bonds of cursed matrimony!
I would not wed again in a thousand years.
Let us women have our hours all our own,
Or. if we mate. give us a husband fool,
Who only sees thro' his fair mistress' eyes."
Now, in the name of heaven, what shall I do?
Hello! what's this? A boy and an old man
Fatigued and sound asleep. Hello, old man!

 O. M.   I pray you. gently. do not waken him!
 Flo.   What business calls you to these lonely parts?
 O. M.   We are in search of Arthur's Knight, Florent.
 Flo.   Well, can you find no trace, no news of him?
 O. M.   Yes, that he lately wandered through these
  parts.
 Jul.   (Awakening.)   O, it is he!—Oh, pardon me
  good father!
For I mistook your face for Knight Florent's,
Whom we have searched for, traveling far and wide.
 Flo.   What is your message to the Knight Florent?

Jul.   The time is brief. He must return to court.
Flo.   (Partly aside.)   Yes, yes, the time is brief,
he must return.
Jul.   But I have news for him of vital moment.
Flo.   What is the news of vital moment, pray?
Jul.   No ears but his must hear the words I have.
They're hidden even from my faithful guide.
Flo.   Good friends, I have a word that will surprise.
If you, old man, wish to proceed and find
In yonder village nourishment and rest,
Within an hour or so I'll find this Knight.
O. M.   How find him, monk?
Flo.   I know his whereabouts.
Jul.   Can we directly find him?
Flo.   Yes.
Jul.   How far?
Flo.   An hour or two will reach him at the most.

Jul.   Kind guide, go on and rest in yonder village.
We'll hasten off to meet this Knight Florent
If, worthy father, you will lead the way.
Flo.   Go with him, Gregory.
O. M.   Farewell.
Jul.   Farewell, we'll reach you presently.
              [Exeunt old man and Gregory. |—R. I.E.
Flo.   Now, boy, what news have you?   I must
explain.
I am his trusted messenger and guide.
You cannot see him, since he is concealed,
Nor can I see him through his messenger.
He only lets me speak.   I have his ear.
His face I have not seen this many a day.
Jul.   You say he is concealed.
Flo.   Yes, yes, he hides.
He is not far ; perhaps a stone's throw off.
Jul.   Oh, where?
Flo.   Somewhat in this direction, here.   (Pointing
towards himself.)
Jul.   Oh, let us go.
Flo.   I dare not, on my word.
Yet I most solemnly devoutly swear,

Upon the faith that clingeth to our order,
I vow eternal secrecy in all;
No other ear shall know except Florent's;
So instantly impart this weighty news.
Your eyes shall never see this Knight Florent.
   Jul. Oh, sir!
   Flo. Why do you weep?
   Jul. Lest some mishap might cut you off, and he
Should never hear.
However, I will briefly tell thee, monk:
The maid for whom Florent is exiled,
Finding the year was drawing to its close,
Raging with fear lest Florent's doom be fixed,
Has made closest inquiry, asking this:
If power divine, or human, or from hell,
Should solve the riddle's knotty mystery.
An aged matron showed to her a way
Well suited to unlock the mystery.
That instant set her youthful soul on fire
To seek the Knight and put her thought to test.
She madly thought to venture forth alone,
Attended only by a single guide.
When I made stout objection to this step,
She trusted all to me and my old guide.
I'd rather die than bring unwelcome news
To that same maid, that Florent was not found.
   Flo. What is the secret she entrusted you?
   Jul. No human skill can solve the mystery.
Solution comes from some dark power below.
   Flo. Then witchcraft must be questioned stealthily.
   Jul. This last resort the matron urged and said,
If you can haply find the errant Knight,
Then bid him hasten to the hills of Wales,
Then seek and climb old Snowden's jagged heights,
Where witches at this season congregate.
The midnight hour is best, and bid him speed.
The time is brief! Let him make speed, be off!
   Flo. A thousand several blessings on that maid!
Oh, if I could but solve this dark enigma
I'd turn my exile to a wedding feast.

If she be dead, I'm doomed a bachelor.
Humbly I'll swear to be her slave forever.
Jul. What do you say?
Flo. What Knight Florent would say
If he had heard the words you lately uttered.
My boy, what say you, will you go with me?
Jul. Most gladly, sir.
Flo. Then you have found your man. I am Florent.
(Throws off his disguise.)
Jul. Oh, sir!
Flo. Be not afraid.
Jul. Oh, sir, my heart!
I feel my heart at times is loosely strung.
Flo. (Sustaining her.) We will partake of food
and rest, then go.
We'll mount provisioned, and seek Snowden's wilds.
But if you fear the journey, fare you well.
Jul. Not I, good Knight Florentius, I will go.
Flo. Then we will hasten, not an instant lost.
We'll question witchcraft at whatever cost.
[Exeunt.]—R. I. E.

Scene II.

Rocky pass in 4. Set rocks R. and L. Region of
Mount Snowden, Wales.
[Thunder and lightning. Florent and Julia enter.]—
R. 3 E.

Jul. How dark, how desolate the way has been!
These heavy mists night-cap old Snowden's top.
Flo. Follow close at my heels. 'Tis fearful dark.
If we should part we might not meet again.
Will you have strength to reach the summit, boy?
Jul. I'll follow you till death.
Flo. Bravo, kind lad! You love this maid,
For love alone can reach such rugged heights.
Jul. I have approved her love this many a year.
From earliest childhood I have known her well.
And now ripe friendship proves the knot most firm.

Flo. Your love is friendship, but mine has no name.

Jul. Yet what is nobler than the love of friend?

Flo. Why, mine, which at its foot o'ershadows
yours.

Jul. Your love is shadow.

Flo. No, 'tis adamant.

Jul. Your love is phantasy.

Flo. 'Tis true as death.

Jul. My love is tried.

Flo. Mine does not need a test.

Jul. What would you do to gain your lady's love?

Flo. I would remove each piece of Snowden's pile,
And fling it in the sea, so she were mine.

Jul. Your Julia should be here to hear you rave.

Flo. I would she were, then I would prove my words.
But boy, I had forgot. what is your name?

Jul. Some call me by one name, some by another.
If you desire it, name me from your love.
Remember, sir, I have been faithful to you.

Flo. By heaven, you have. A thousand thanks for
that!

Jul. You see, too, I am somewhat of her height.
You see, sir, I have something of her features.
I've often heard I am her very image.
To soften these hard hours, then, call me Julia.
Were I in maiden raiment now attired,
You would at moments truly think me Julia.

Flo. Oh, would I could one moment think you Julia.
This night were day, and I in Arthur's Court.

Jul. I'll keep this habit, but assume I'm she.
I know her every motion. look and sigh.
I know I'll play the part most perfectly.
When we return to good King Arthur's court
I'll find for thee not only home, but Julia,
If haply this night's quest be not in vain.

Flo. We'll bear up in the thundering pelting storm,
Earthquake or hurricane shall not obstruct us.
We'll tramp old Snowden till the riddle's solved.
I strangely long for midnight's dreadful hour,

And sudden boldness pricks at every nerve.
A strange, unwonted feeling telleth me,
That this same hour shall show us wondrous sights.

Jul. Oh, may the sight direct us to the light!

Flo. Come, let us go.

Jul. I'm ready. Knight, proceed.

Flo. Cast frequent glances on the clifts below.
I'll watch the summit for every flitting thing.

Jul. Nothing shall pass us. Shadows, the thick clouds,
The very air I'll boldly hail and question.

Flo. My lad, you have a heart that is all man.
We'll range the mountain and invade these hags.

    [Leave.]
    [Thunder and lightning.]—L. 3 E.
    [A witch passes over the stage. Then
    another.]

Flo. (Entering.) Hello, ho! Boy, hello! Where are you?- (Exit.)
    [A company of witches enter with Julia.]—R.

Jul. Come, hags, if you will solve this riddle for me,
Ask what you will within my power and I
Will grant it you.
    [Witches go to side, confer and return.]

1 W. We'll solve this riddle, if you will join our band and take the vows of witchcraft.

Jul. Must I join your band and verily become a witch?

1 W. You must become a witch to solve this riddle.

Jul. Is there any release from witchcraft? Could I ever become a maid again?

1 W. Never, unless a Knight would woo you as a witch, plight his troth to you as a witch, bestow the ring upon your witch's finger, and seal the engagement with a kiss upon your witch's lips. and when the marriage ceremony is performed, it must be public. in the presence of the court, both Knights and Ladies, and some King must tie the knot. Nor dare you disclose to your betrothed this secret and key to your redemption, for, if you violate our code of witchcraft, you are accursed forever, and never can return to maidenhood.

Jul. 'Tis a hard bargain, witches!
If ye will not disclose this secret to me.
Will ye not disclose it to this valiant Knight?

1 W. Never! We and all of our kind stand accursed in his code of chivalry! We'll grant no favors to an enemy.

[Julia goes to side and weeps. Returns.]

Jul. Must I make this mighty sacrifice, and hang my hopes of earth and heaven upon so slender a thread? (Weeps.)

1 W. You must become a witch to solve this riddle.

Jul. Then practice your hellish arts, compound your drugs,
Prepare your potent charm and invoke hell.
If you will show what women most desire
I'll join your band, forever follow you.

Witches. Good! Good!

Jul. Unless a noble Knight will marry me; (Witches laugh.)
Yes, I have sworn I'll marry none save him. (Witches laugh.)

2 W. I've hunted one this hundred years.

1 W. Thou fool!
When earth shall bump the sun you'll find a mate.

2 W. And you when hell is frozen shore to shore.

Jul. I have one more condition which heed well,
That you will not disclose this to Florent.
Howe'er he plead, you shall not answer him.
The secret's mine alone. What say you, hags?

1 W. Thy offer we approve. Lay thine arm bare.

Jul. What will you do?

1 W. My blood and thine must mingle?

Jul. My word's enough.

1 W. Blood showeth thee sincere.

Jul. Then draw it quickly.

1 W. Baubo, fetch the cup.
Come, Lilith, strike!

Jul. How painless, quick and red!

> [Baubo catches the blood in the crown of a skull.]

B. Enough!

Lil. Then cease to flow, and vanish spot.

1 W. Now touch thy lips.

Jul. I drink,

1 W. I bid thee speed.

> [The witches all round her bow to the very ground.]

All. We are thy slaves until thy work be done.

> [1 W. beats time; the witches dance about her hand in hand to weird music.]

1 W. Come, come, join hands and round her speed.
Tell earth and air and hell the deed,
Another soul has joined our crew!

> [Wildly gesticulating upward and then downward.]

Hurrah! Shoohoo! Owow! Shoohoo!

All. [Suddenly stop dancing and with similar gestures.]

Hurrah! Shoohoo! Owow! Shoohoo!

1 W. (All dancing again.) Thou spirit of the nether night,
Up in the mountains speed thou light;
Let witchcraft's work be quickly through!

> [Standing with arms above her head and whirling in her place rapidly, then throwing out her arms repeatedly, as if drawing in a line.]

Hurrah! Shoohoo! Owow! Shoohoo!

> [All do the same and continue as in act of drawing in a line, until it thunders and lightnings.]

1 W. Enough, enough! The spirit's nigh!
Now form the charm! Around her fly!
> [They whirl hand in hand about her with
> the utmost speed.]

Once! Twice! Thrice!
> [Wildly gesticulating.]

Up, show thyself and quickly pass!
> [Thunder and lightning.]

Jul. What's this?
> [An apparition of a woman holding a
> crown passes quickly over the stage.]

Enough, enough, I understand!
> [The witches come to Julia to congratu-
> late her, slapping her on the shoul-
> der, shaking her hand violently,
> pulling her about, laughing, jeering,
> screeching, hopping about, etc. They
> besmear her face and throw over her
> a witch's cloak and cap.]

1 W. Now sisters, for the dance!—

VERSE I.

Hurrah, join. form the devil's reel!
Hurrah, shout, stamp, mark toe and heel.
All in the circle panting.
Now, strike to left.
Now kick to right.
Now each one for the center fight.
And screech ow, ow, and yell shoohoo, shoohoo!
Shoohoo, owow, shoohoo!

VERSE II.

Squeak witches' music by the yard,
Fortissimo, allegro, bard!
All jeering and careering.
Now oil your toes
With witches' lard!
Fly up, fly down, now soft, now hard!
And screech owow, and yell shoohoo, shoohoo!
Shoohoo! Owow! Shoohoo!
> [Thunder and lightning.]

Flo. (R. 3 E. Entering) Ho, boy, ho! Hello boy,
help ho! —
[Witches all suddenly stop dancing.
Lightning.]
Ha! Here they are! Good evening all. I find a
merry company. I pray you do not let me interrupt
your mirth.

1 W. What brings you such a distance, Knight?

Flo. I follow a most difficult quest.

1 W. What is your quest?

Flo. I seek to know what it is that women love the
best.

1 W. That is easily done.
(With gestures): What women trow
To love the best
The Knight would know.
Thy power I'll test.
Now quickly show.
(Tableau of gold, jewelry, etc.)

Flo. Gold, omnipotent gold, monarch of all mon-
archs,—what mean you, that everything may be bought
and sold, that every man and woman is purchasable?
I tell you plainly I do not like your picture. There is
a rarer jewel than any yonder, the jewel that sparkles
from the eye and binds two hearts together.
(Tableau, two lovers.)
What's this, a fond couple, bound together in the
eternal bonds of love? What, have I a choice or are
you deluding me?
(Tableau, the devil.)
[Witches all scream.]
Fiends, death and damnation light on you! (Draws.)
[Thunder and lightning. Witches disap-
pear. Julia remains behind. |

Flo. I'll hold brief converse with you. Stop, I
pray!

Jul. What do you seek on Snowden's rocky
heights?
Is your way lost, or what is your distress?
Ah, by your face I see your mind's disturbed.
Speak Knight, we hags are bound to serve your sex.

Flo. You guess aright. My doom is well nigh
    sealed.
It is decreed that I shall be exiled
Unless I find what women most desire.
I've wandered far and wide and questioned thousands.
The long and dreary year I've searched and suffered,
And now, I am no nearer to my goal.
Help, grand dame, help! If thou wilt solve the riddle,
Ask what thou wilt and I will give it thee.

Jul. Grant me then quickly that thou'lt marry me,
And I'll assure thee, by dread witchcraft's power,
My answer'll satisfy all of our sex.
Both maids and wives and widows shall agree.

Flo. Speak not in sport.
Jul. I speak most earnestly.
Flo. Joke not, hag.
Jul. Do you not hear my words?
Flo. How old art thou? (Patting her under the
chin.)
Jul. I'm not an hour old.
Flo. Foul hag, thou liest!
Jul. Did witchcraft ever lie?
Flo. You stayed behind, I now perceive, to mock.
Jul. I stayed behind to save thee from exile.
Flo. It were the foullest death to marry thee.
Jul. That thou must do to save thee from exile.
Flo. (Aside.) If I can once extract the answer
 .   from her,
Surely the queen will not compel this match.—
Well, thou hast conquered me at last, my crone.
Thy offer I'll accept, and I am thine.

Jul. Then hand me the engagement ring.
Flo. Here 'tis.
Jul. Now seal it with a kiss.
Flo. Oh, Lord!
Jul. Come, love!
Flo. Here 'tis.
Jul. There then.
Flo. You do not kiss like a witch.

Jul. I swear you'll kiss me with a relish, yet.
Our contract sealed I will fulfill my vow.
Now whither wilt thou go?
 Flo. To Arthur's court.
 Jul. We will proceed and fear not on the way.
We'll find thy steed, a devil will lead the way.
Haste, mount thy horse, I'll sit close at thy side.
As we advance, I'll teach thee what to say.
 Flo. I've lost a comrade somewhere in these wilds,
Let us find him, I pray, before we start.
 Jul. Mean'st thou a lad, called Julia, from the
  king?
He'll be at Camelot, when you arrive.
So come, make haste, already I see your fate.
We'll reach the court before it is too late.
   [Florent and Julia go up run to platform.
    Witches re-enter and form tableau. |
    Curtain.

ACT IV.

Apartment of Female Court.   Curtains in rear.
[Florent and Julia enter.]—L. I. E.

Jul.   Now left alone, one fond embrace. (She
  embraces him.)

Flo.   Oh Death!   (Breaks away.)
Keep thy accursed claws from off my body.
Accursed lot!   Keep off, and not a word.

Jul.   Why not a word?

Flo.   I say my mouth is closed.

Jul.   Nay, be not angry, be not vexed my dear,
And husband, but pronounce my fault.

Flo.   Not I.   (Turns his back.)

Jul.   Tell me wherein I am to blame.

Flo.   Not I.

Jul.   Come, let me take you in my arms!

Flo.   Not I.   (Moves away.   She follows him.)

Jul.   Come, come, be not so shy!   One arm I beg!
    [She slips one arm about him and puts
        one of his about her.]
Now tell me, dear, why is it you are sad?

Flo.   (Shudders.)   You are so old, so homely,
  withered, black.
Jack Lechery could not be moved by you.

Jul.   And is that all, my dearest, sweetest man?

Flo.   And is that not enough?   Have you not heard
That man should take a younger for a spouse?
And I to-day must mate my great granddame.

Jul.   And is this all, beloved spouse?   Speak on!

Flo.   And you are sprung from such accursed stock.

Jul.   Have you not heard that we are sprung from
  heaven?

Flo.   You know you were born and brought up in
  hell.

Jul. No, no, my lord, for we precede dame Eve.
And are the first that Adam did compound.
His first wife, Lilith, gave us birth. 'Tis true!
And Eve is but our aged step-mother.
You have the fairer outward show, I know,
But we are inward mightier far than you.
What would the world without us witches be?
  (One arm around his neck and takes his hand.)
 Flo. (Breaks away.) Stop! Shall I love the devil
  against my will?
 Jul. (Follows him.) The devil is not half so bad
  a fellow
As idlers urge and sinners loudly bellow.
Not thoughtlessly the Eternal dropped this weed,
To rear you lazy Knights for manly deeds,
And lets the Devil sprout for all eternity.
For the Devil's true name is Sir Necessity.
And not to shun this prince, is our salvation.
Naught ails the Devil save his reputation.
He's born to be affronted and amused.
The bold are saved but cowards are abused.
Up, challenge him, and fight and godlike grow!
Only through Satan can we heavenward go!
 Flo. You tire me from foot to very crown.
Satan and women never can run down.
 Jul. You know but little of women and the devil.
(Taking his hand.) Long, long years hence, when
  we are bent with age,
When children grown shall guide our tottering steps,
We'll go together at the beck of death.
But now, rejoice, dear Knight, we soon are one.
  (Kisses F.)
 Flo. Were it not for your age, your stock, your
  face,
Your shrewish temper with a restless tongue,
I might resign me to a fate like this.
But though I see you love me, flattering hag,
And have a reason I cannot rebut,
I tell you plainly I'll not wed alive.
    [Exit Florent followed by Jul.]—L. 2 E.
    [Vivien and Catherine enter.]—R. 2 E.
 Cath. Think you there is a servant in the kingdom
so ill paid as I for this vile work?

Viv. (Gives a coin.) Here. Is there any one about? Look behind that curtain. (C. steps to curtain and opens slightly while Vivien looks out at the sides.)

Cath. No, there is no one here. (Looks at the coin and smiles.)

Viv. Why do you smile? Here, take this. (Gives her another coin.) Does that stop your fault-finding mouth?

Cath. Stop my mouth? Nay, my mouth would hold a basket full of such as this.

Viv. Here, shrivel-heart, for your ingratitude. (Throws a handful of coin at C.'s feet. C. picks them up.)

Cath. Now you are coming to your senses; for, of the bold and reckless undertakings of my day, yours eclipses them all. Your attempt to forge Guinevere's handwriting in that book was such a clumsy effort that—

Viv. Yet, it worked perfectly!

Cath. The queen's testimony will—

Viv. Will be of no avail. She is the party accused. Whoever heard of an accused person testifying in favor of herself.

Cath. Then the Knight's testimony will—

Viv. Will never be heard. He will never again show his face in Camelot!

Cath. But this forged note which the king has in his possession?

Viv. Who will be able to prove the knight's hand if the knight is absent?

Cath. And the handkerchief which you contrived to get from Florent—

Viv. I understand!

Cath. On the plea that you had lost yours—

Viv. Yes, yes, yes, why so explicit about all these things? You talk just as if there was somebody listening, while you explain this matter. (Starts for the curtain.)

Cath. In your mad recklessness to dethrone Guinevere—

Viv For heaven's sake, not so loud!

Cath. —and place the crown upon your head, you have resorted to means not only most despicable, but the most rash! (Vivien forces a laugh.) First, you poison the ears of the king by a thousand little acts inciting his jealousy,—

Viv. Well—

Cath. —then you pour a stream of falsehood into the knight's ears to make him believe that the queen loves him.—

Viv. Well,—

Cath. —then you find the queen and tell her the knight is desperately in love with her.

Viv. Well, well,—

Cath. You get up a flirtation, the King takes it most seriously and well nigh runs mad with jealousy.—

Viv. Yes, but what are you—

Cath. Then you forge a note—

Viv. (Trembling.) Great God. I thought I saw the curtain move. (Greatly excited.)

Cath. You are somewhat nervous. But, 'tis likely, though, for the windows are open letting in the breeze.

Viv. Heavens! What a fright that gave me! (Sinks into chair.)

Cath. You give him credit for a vast deal of shrewdness—indeed you do! (Vivien rises.)

Viv. Why, Catherine, it will astonish you to see what complete control I have of Arthur, twisting him about my finger at will.

Cath. He is a man of too noble a character to be dealt with thus.

Viv. Ah, yes, a noble blockhead!

Cath. He certainly has judgment and discernment.

Viv. A wee bit, enough to keep him warm.

Cath. He is a splendid specimen of knightly valor.

Viv. And needs a shrewd woman behind the throne. You see, I have taken pity on him. When Vivien is queen, we'll have another Arthur.

Cath. So be it, but I have my doubts about the success of your—

Viv. Have no fears! He is more easily imposed upon than any of his Knights.

Cath. So you are marrying a man whom you cannot even respect, much less love?

Viv. I am not marrying the man, I am marrying the king. I shall furnish the brains and let him furnish the love. I think I can endure the union, provided there are gems enough in my crown, and provided he does not live too long. (Nudging her) Some day I can find a younger man more to my taste.

[King and queen come out from behind curtain C.]

King. Go find him now! (Vivien staggers back.) I think a dungeon is the meetest place for her! (Vivien sinks into a chair, rises again.)

Queen. Drive her from the court! That is enough for me. (V. trembles, makes a dash at Catherine, then staggers back and slowly withdraws L.) Farewell thou gilded infidelity!

King. Come, let us celebrate our second marriage. (Kisses queen.)

[SONG.]

Let others, ogle maids, admire 'em,
Love the fair damsels, wint and fool 'em,
But as for me, my bonny m'stress,
Her, her alone will I kiss and caress!
My lilly of Britain, my peerless queen,
My wife, my wife, my wife,
Will do for me!
So lovers attend :—
All true lovers be,
And come to some good end!

Now, if your wife have a freckle or two,
Freckles are nil when the heart is true.
A bit of powder will make her fair,
And chemicals will freshen her hair.
Call her your lilly, call her your queen,
Your wife, your wife, your wife,
Will do for you!
So, lovers attend :—
All be lovers true,
And come to some good end!

Now, married men who dare to roam
From their sweet wives, when away from home,
Out, out on such rogues! No scullions for me!
None, none but my merry spouse will I see!
My lilly of Britain, my matchless queen,

My wife, my wife, my wife,
Will do for me!
So lovers attend :—
Who false lovers be,
Will come to some bad end! (All leave R. 2 E.)

[Julia opens and stands between parted curtains.]
Here is the room, the hour, the spot.
This narrow space decides my lot.
Within this box, this hole, this nitche,
Free is the Knight, entrapped the witch!
Crushed and destroyed all witchcraft's power
If he's not mine within an hour!
He'll smartly sweat for all my pain,
But then rejoice in double gain.
(Closes and steps back.)
[Enter King, Queen and Court R.]
[Messenger enters.]—.L I. E.
Guin.. What news?
Mess. Your Knight Florent has returned to Camelot.
He waits your bidding at the door, and humbly asks
To presently appear before the Court.
And rumor hath it he came not alone,
But slinked in ere the dawn beside a witch
As black and filthy as contagion.
There is some mystery wrapped in her weeds.
This day may see strange visages and deeds.
Guin. Bid him enter.
1st Lady. The valiant Knight is here.
What answer think you?
2nd Lady. Are we to be the jury?
Guin. We must all pass judgment. Here comes
the Knight!
[Enter Florentius.]—L. I. E.
Welcome, good Knight Florent, we honor you
That you have come so close upon the hour
When you were bid to answer our decree.
Now, without further words, I bid you speak.
Your answer give, what women strive for most.
Flo. Most noble Queen,
What women most desire is sovereignty.
The man must be the puppet, you must reign,
Make every beck and look and turn your gain.
When at the altar's fragrant step we're found,

You hold our soul in feof, when once we're bound.
You women all do stoutly strive to rule.
'Tis vainly thought by many a dull brained fool
The strength of boasting man bends all things to it.
'Tis all illusion! Woman 'tis shines through it.
You would be masters; we but slaves forever.
For man's a rogue, and mastery suits him never.

Guin.   I must confess, your wit is strangely shrewd.
1st Lady.   He is inspired!
2nd Lady.   'Tis wonderful!
3rd Lady.   'Tis true!
Guin.   What say the rest? Are all agreed?
Ladies.   We are!
Guin.   Knight, we discharge you, you are free to go.
Flo.   My benefactor, gracious Queen, I thank you!
(Kneels.)

(Kisses her hand and starts to leave.)
Jul.   (Coming forward.) Stop, sir, another benefactor speaks!
Most worthy King, 'twas I that taught the Knight
What answer he should give to your demand,
And he has firmly plighted me his troth. (Shows
ring.)
I now demand fulfillment of his vow.
King.   What do you say, Florentius, to the hag?
Flo.   I do confess, most worthy King, 'tis true,
But hope you will not press me to this match.
King.   You promised by your faith to wed this
crone?
Flo.   Yes, but you will not force this union, King;
Although my lips were bold to sanction it,
It came not from my heart, most worthy King.
Jul.   Your heart or not, you promised to marry me.
Flo.   Should I, earth-born, wed you?
Jul.   Yes, prudently.
Flo.   No, no, old woman!
King.   Did you not, Knight, yourself make her your
wife?
Flo.   It was an evil hour! I curse it, King!
King.   You have consented. Her appeal is just.
Flo.   Nay, pity me, and think you, what a fate!
King.   She's your salvation, Knight, and 'tis too
late.
Flo.   You will not force me to embrace this hag?

I much prefer quick death! Take thou my life!
I'll never marry this mad, withered crone!
   King. Arthur decrees that you shall marry her.
   Flo. Come, hag. if you'll pronounce me this day free,
My goods, my lands, aught else I own are yours!
   Jul. I scorn your pelf, your unaffected gold!
A richer treasure I shall find in you.
   Flo. I'll pay you worthy tribute while I live.
   Jul. I'll live upon the tribute of your love.
   Flo. (Falls at her feet.) Then let me live your
     slave, but not your husband!
   Jul. (Her hand on his head.) You'll be my hus-
     band in about one minute.
(To the King.) We are ready!
   King. Well. Knight, arise! Now, bride and groom
     join hands.
     (He gets up; they join hands.)
Now. wilt thou take this woman, Knight Florent?
   Flo. (Throwing away her hand.) Oh, king, I
     love but one! Her name is Julia.
My life is naught unless I marry her.
I loved her from the moment I first saw her.
'Tis death itself to make me wed the hag.
     (Ladies gather to one side and talk earnestly.)
   King. I say, join hands, as I have bidden you.
   Ladies. Shame! shame! The poor Knight! Have
     pity, have mercy!
     (Crowding around the King.)
   King. I have decreed that he shall marry her.
Now. wilt thou take this woman, Sir Knight Florent?
   Flo. Against my will and better fate, I do. (Takes
     her hand.)
   King. What is your name?
   Jul. My name is Julia, sir.
   Flo. (Flinging away her hand.) Heaven's light-
     nings blast thy cursed lips for that!
'Tis not enough that I should marry her,
But she must mock me with the name I love.
   King. Her wit is somewhat shrewd, the more your gain.
Knight, we will not dispute about the name.
Now. Julia, will you take this man to wed?
   Jul. With all my heart, I'll take him for all time.
And him I'll make all happiest of men.

King.   Then, I pronounce you man and wife forever.
Jul.   Now, Knight, before one unkind word shall
  pass,
Of two things which I may possess you of,
I'll freely make my offer.   You take one.
Now, shall I give you beauty, grace and form,
One of the fairest forms the sex contains,
A wife possessed of all the female charms,
And yet possessed of all their frailties,
Perhaps as fickle as Helena of Troy?
Or, will you, on the other hand, have me
As I am now, old, withered, black and bent,
Yet rid of all the vices of my sex,
Your dear, affectionate, tender, loving spouse,
Your most obedient slave, in all things true,
The very essence of fidelity,
To worship, live and die but for her lord?
Speak, Florent, husband, choose!   You have your
  choice.
  Flo.   My lord, she claims that by dread witchcraft's
  power
She can transform her being as she wills;
To be a perfect beauty, or a crone.
I am afraid to face the cunning hag.
  Jul.   Well, husband, what's your choice?
      (Behind him with her hand on his shoulder.)
  Flo.   I leave the choice with you, you know the best.
  Jul.   Well, Knight Florent, since you are turned
    the wife,
Since I am now your husband and your lord,
Since you repose some judgment in a woman,
And grant us sovereignty at last,
I'll give you all I have, and that is both,
I'll give both beauty and fidelity.   (Throwing off her
    veil and cloak.)
I am your loving, most obedient wife.
And I am he that showed you to Mount Snowden.
When there, I thought I'd join the witches for you.
  Flo.   I've found my lad, my witch, my wife, my Julia!
She has more pluck than any man in town!
Let women wear the trousers, man the gown!
The female head's the head deserves the crown.
          Curtain.

www.ingramcontent.com/pod-product-compliance
Lightning Source LLC
Chambersburg PA
CBHW031807090426
42739CB00008B/1205